Our WILD™ WORLD

SERIES

Orangutans

NORTHWORD PRESS

Chanhassen, Minnesota

DEDICATION
For Kenny and Mindy
– D.D.

© NorthWord Press, 2003

Photography © 2003: Anup Shah: cover, pp. 4, 13, 15, 16-17, 18, 20, 23, 26, 29, 30-31, 32-33, 34, 36-37, 40; Erwin & Peggy Bauer: pp. 5, 43; Kevin Schafer/kevinschafer.com: p. 6; Adam Jones: p. 9; Anup Shah/Dembinsky Photo Associates: pp. 10-11, back cover; Konrad Wothe/Minden Pictures: pp. 14, 38-39; D. Robert & Lorri Franz: p. 19; Frans Lanting/Minden Pictures: pp. 25, 44.

Illustrations by John F. McGee
Designed by Russell S. Kuepper
Edited by Judy Gitenstein

NorthWord Press
18705 Lake Drive East
Chanhassen, MN 55317
1-800-328-3895
www.northwordpress.com

Library of Congress Cataloging-in-Publication Data

Dennard, Deborah.
    Orangutans / Deborah Dennard ; illustrations by John McGee.
        p.   cm.   – (Our wild world series)
    Summary: Discusses the physical characteristics, behavior, habitat, and life cycle of orangutans.
    ISBN 1-55971-848-X (hardcover) – ISBN 1-55971-847-1 (softcover)
        1. Orangutan—Juvenile literature. [1. Orangutan.] I. McGee, John F., ill. II. Title.
    III. Series.

    QL737.P96 D463 2003
    599.883—dc21

                                                                    2002032636

Printed in Malaysia

10 9 8 7 6 5 4 3 2 1

Orangutans

Deborah Dennard
Illustrations by John F. McGee

NorthWord Press
Chanhassen, Minnesota

ORANGUTANS are mysterious creatures. The people of Malay (ma-LAY), which is now known as Malaysia, called the creature *orang hutan* (oh-RANG WHO-tan). This means "old man of the forest." There is a legend about how the orangutan got its name. The story is about a man who owed his neighbors some money.

When he could not pay the money back, he hid in the forest. He stayed there so long he became more like the animals of the forest and less like a human. As the legend goes, after a long time his children came to be orangutans. Other Malayan people believed that orangutans were simply another tribe of unusual people.

Some native people in Malaysia believed that orangutans were simply odd-looking people who lived in trees.

This mother Bornean orangutan will spend 7 years taking care of her baby.

Male orangutans, such as this Borean male, have fleshy cheek pads that frame their faces and make their heads look large and round.

Orangutans are very unusual. They are the largest arboreal (ar-BOR-ee-al) animals in the world. Arboreal animals live mostly in trees.

Male orangutans weigh 200 to 300 pounds (90-136 kilograms) and are twice as big as females. They are about 5 feet (1.5 meters) tall and have very long arms, short legs, and long hands. Their arm span, the distance from one hand to another with their arms outstretched, may be as wide as 8 feet (2.5 meters). They have bright, red-orange shaggy fur.

Males have fleshy half circles on their cheeks that are called cheek disks or pads. These pads frame the face and make orangutans' heads seem to be very large. The pads are a sign of adulthood. The larger the cheek pad, the more important the orangutan is. To some people, this makes orangutans look very strange.

Orangutans
FUNFACT:

The natives of Borneo (BORE-nee-oh) told stories of orangutans that were so strong they could stand on top of a crocodile and hold its jaws open!

Orangutans live only on the Southeast Asian islands of Sumatra (left)
and Borneo (right), shown in the red areas above.

Orangutans may live to be about 40 years old in the wild. Orangutans once lived throughout Southeast Asia. Now they only live on the Southeast Asian islands of Borneo and Sumatra (Sue-MA-tra). Orangutans from Borneo and Sumatra are separated by the open waters between their islands. Though there are differences between these orangutans, they are still very much alike. They could breed and have babies together. Because of this, scientists call them subspecies. That means they are almost, but not quite, exactly alike.

The scientific name for orangutans is *Pongo pygmaeus*.

Bornean orangutans, like the male shown here,
have thinner hair than Sumatran orangutans.

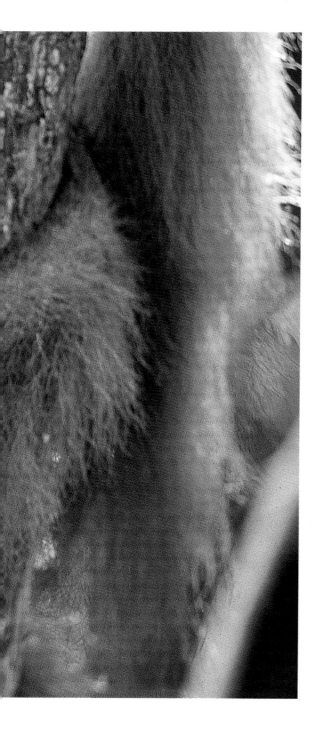

Orangutans on Sumatra have thicker fur than the orangutans on Borneo. Scientists think the reason may be that it is colder on Sumatra, and orangutans there need more fur to keep them warm. Sumatran orangutans have thin, diamond-shaped faces, orange mustaches (mus-TASH-es), and a small throat sac. Bornean orangutans have larger, rounder cheek pads, a square shaped face, and a very large throat sac. The throat sac allows an orangutan's neck to expand. This lets more air through and makes their calls louder.

The closest relatives of orangutans are gorillas and chimpanzees, but they do not look much alike. However, all three are so closely related they belong to the same family, the family of great apes.

Orangutans' feet are as useful as their hands for gripping things.

All great apes are primates (PRY-mates). It is easy to tell if an animal is a primate. First of all, primates are mammals. Mammals are animals that have hair and are able to nurse their babies, or feed them milk from their bodies. A primate also has opposable (uh-POE-zih-bull) thumbs. An opposable thumb can reach across the palm of the hand for picking up things.

Orangutans have long hands and fingers and short thumbs that work like hooks. Orangutans also have opposable big toes. This allows them to climb, travel, and hang in trees.

Primates have eyes that face forward on their faces. They have large heads and brains. Primates are very intelligent creatures. Orangutans, like monkeys, gorillas, chimpanzees, and humans, are primates.

Like all primates, orangutans have opposable thumbs.

Orangutans live in different habitats. A habitat is a type of environment where an animal lives. An orangutan's habitat can be a tropical rain forest, a swamp forest, or a high tropical mountain forest. There are perhaps only 25,000 orangutans left in the wild. The rest live in zoos.

Orangutans
FUNFACT:

Orangutans are the only great apes that live in Asia and the only great ape to spend most of their time in trees.

Orangutans live in wet, green places like rain forests and swamp forests. They get most of the water they need from the food they eat, but like this young one, they may come down to a stream for a drink.

This orangutan is chewing on a long, green plant stalk, but fruit is the biggest part of the orangutan diet.

Orangutans love to eat fruit. In fact, they are the largest animals in the world to depend on fruit as the most important part of their diet. Scientists have identified about 400 different types of food in an orangutan's diet. More than half of their diet is fruit. A favorite wild food of orangutans comes from the durian (DUR-ee-en) tree. The fruit tastes like sugar and garlic, and is creamy like a pudding. Orangutans also eat leaves, flowers, bark, nuts, and sometimes even eggs. They also eat small animals and insects, such as lizards and caterpillars. Because they eat both meat and plants, they are omnivores (OM-ni-vorz). Meat makes up a very small part of an orangutan's diet, though. It is not nearly as important to them as fruit.

15

How do orangutans find enough food in the forest to survive? They find food in different parts of the same tall trees. Because female orangutans are half the size of male orangutans, they can climb higher in the trees. That is where they find their food. Male orangutans are so large they cannot climb very high in the trees. They stay lower down in the trees, and that is where they find their food. Rain forest trees can grow to be 100 feet tall (about 30 meters). Males and females can share these same tall trees but never notice each other, except when it is time to breed. Eating in different parts of trees is a way to make sure that all the orangutans get enough to eat.

Orangutans
FUNFACT:

Orangutans do not need to go to the ground to find water. They drink rain that has collected in hollows and holes in the tree branches.

This mother orangutan and her baby are smaller than male orangutans, so they can climb higher in trees to look for food.

Orangutans travel across the same routes in the forest. They have a very good memory for the location of fruit trees and visit them over and over again. Males may travel as many as 3 miles (4.8 kilometers) in a single day to find food. Females are smaller than males, and they need less food. They stay closer to home and only travel about 1 mile (1.6 kilometers) in a day.

Scientists believe that orangutans are able to remember many details about their forest homes. They can remember where good feeding trees are and the seasons when fruits will be ripe. Orangutans do not just wander through the jungle trying to find fruit trees. They seem to head to certain areas and trees at just the right time. This helps to show how intelligent orangutans are. They have map-like memories of the forests.

Orangutans use their strong, long arms and legs to travel across the routes they know well in the forest. They seem to remember certain trees and when their fruit will be ripe.

Finding enough food is important. Orangutans must eat a great deal of food to feed their large bodies. They may spend half of each day eating, and the other half resting. Sometimes several orangutans gather together, especially if there is a tree with a lot of fruit on it. As many as 8 orangutans have been seen feeding together, but this is very rare.

Orangutans do not appear to be in a hurry. They eat slowly and usually alone. They climb slowly through the tall trees of the forest. Scientists used to think that their slow pace meant they were not intelligent. This is not true. Instead, it helps orangutans to survive. For example, their slow movement is one way orangutans avoid predators (PRED-uh-torz). Because they sit still for long periods and move slowly, orangutans can blend safely into the forest.

This young Sumatran orangutan is old enough to explore on his own but has not yet become an adult.

Scientists used to think that orangutans stayed away from water, but some orangutans, including this young one, seek out water and even play in it.

Orangutans in captivity have helped scientists learn how intelligent these animals are. Like gorillas and chimpanzees, they can learn sign language. They have been known to pick the locks of their cages and always seem interested in what their keepers are doing. They explore the world around them by touching, tasting, and smelling things. Orangutans in the wild have even been known to steal people's backpacks just to have a look inside!

Scientists used to think that orangutans were afraid of water, but this is not completely true. Some orangutans plunge right into jungle streams. Others go out of their way to cross at the shallowest part of the streams. Different orangutans act in different ways around water. Some young orangutans even seem to play in the water.

Orangutans
FUNFACT:

Some orangutans in captivity have learned as many as 150 words in sign language.

Orangutans need good balance to climb high in the rain forest trees. This is no problem, even for 200-pound (90-kilogram) males. Their strong legs and arms are perfect for climbing and balancing.

Orangutans are so strong they can support their entire body weight with any one hand or foot. Their hands are rough and calloused from climbing in the trees, and they can use their feet the same way they use their hands.

Their shoulder joints and hip joints are very strong and flexible. This allows orangutans to stretch and reach for branches. They seem to have no fear of heights and no problem hanging upside down.

Orangutans
FUNFACT:

Orangutans can even eat while hanging upside down.

Orangutans are strong and climb equally well with their hands and feet.

A mother orangutan uses her body like a bridge so that
her baby can cross safely between two trees.

Orangutans move through the trees using their long arms, their long hook-like hands, and their grasping feet. They do not swing quickly between the trees like some other primates do. Instead, they use their arms and legs to bend one tree branch to meet another. This forms a bridge that they can use to climb through the trees. Sometimes an orangutan will even rock back and forth in a tree, causing the tree to bend far enough to reach the next tree.

A mother orangutan with young may use her body to make a bridge. She holds onto one tree with her hands and another tree with her feet. As she closes the gap between the trees, her youngster simply scampers across her back.

It might seem that orangutans find safety in the treetops. This is not always true. In Sumatra, clouded leopards share the treetops with orangutans. These strong predators usually leave large male orangutans alone. However, leopards hunting in the trees sometimes catch sleeping female orangutans. Sometimes large snakes may kill baby orangutans, but predators do not present too much of a danger to most orangutans.

Orangutans in Borneo are more likely to come down to the ground than orangutans in Sumatra. The reason is that there are no tigers in Borneo, so there is safety on the ground. They also may come down to the ground more often because the forest in Borneo is not as thick as the forest in Sumatra. They have to come down to the ground to get from one place to another.

Most orangutans spend most of their lives high in the treetops. This baby seems to be playing as it climbs in a tree.

Very long arms and legs help orangutans to stretch from one tree branch to another and to reach a long way to grab fruit.

Sumatran orangutans spend as much as 95 percent of their lives in the trees because of the thick forests there and because of the danger of tigers. It may sometimes take longer to move around in the trees than on the ground, but for orangutans in Sumatra, it is usually safer in the trees.

Orangutans on the ground do not move around very well, and they walk with their feet curled into fists. The heels of their feet are not well suited for walking flat-footed. They are slower and clumsier on the ground than in the trees. However, some orangutans seem to like it better on the ground. One male orangutan was known to spend as many as 6 hours a day on the ground. Some large males even make nests on the ground. Still, most orangutans spend most of their time in the trees.

One advantage of life in the trees for orangutans is the camouflage (KAM-uh-flaj) of their bright orange fur. It may seem that their fur would be easy to spot in the trees, but it is not. With the bright sunlight and the dark shade caused by the huge trees, orangutan fur blends right into the treetops. Their fur looks a lot like the trees and the plants that grow on the trees.

Orangutans
FUNFACT:

Baby orangutans have light orange fur and pink or white patches of skin around their eyes.

Most primates are social animals and live in groups. Orangutans are different. They spend most of their lives alone. The only exception is a mother orangutan. She may spend 7 or more years caring for a single youngster. Of all primates, only humans spend more time caring for their young.

Although orangutans live alone, their territories overlap. Within the territory of each male there are usually about 4 females. Each female lives alone or with her baby, but away from the male. Females may call softly to their babies, but these calls are not nearly as loud as the calls of males.

Males announce their territory daily with loud, echoing calls. These "long calls" sound something like the roar of a lion and are made louder by the male orangutan's throat sac. This sac inflates to make a stronger sound. The long call can be heard more than a mile away.

Smaller male orangutans know to stay away from these calls because they announce the territory of a stronger, larger male. Females with babies also stay away, but females without babies are attracted by these calls. The long calls may be a way orangutans find each other in the dense forest at mating time.

Except when mother orangutans are caring for their babies, most orangutans spend much of their lives alone.

Males sometimes fight. They show sharp teeth, bite, and wrestle each other, especially when a female is near.

Sometimes when a female without a baby is near two males, the males fight over the female. They bite and wrestle. Orangutans are so strong that gashes and broken bones from biting and wrestling are common. Orangutans also break off tree branches and throw them to the ground when they fight. They show their irritation by making loud, sharp, sucking noises called "kiss squeaks."

Males show off for females at mating time. Hanging upside down in a tree and making long calls is a favorite thing for males to do to get females' attention. Females like this. The males that please females are the ones most likely to father new babies.

Male orangutans in Borneo stay with their females for only a few days when mating. In Sumatra the males stay with their females for several months until the baby is born. They make sure the mother gets enough food.

A pregnant female is about 50 pounds (23 kilograms) heavier than a female that is not pregnant. This makes it hard to move in the trees and find food. Without a male to scare away other animals, a Sumatran female may have a hard time getting enough food. After the baby is born, the female is lighter. She can move around more easily in the trees to find fruit so the male goes his own way.

An orangutan baby takes about 8.5 months to grow inside its mother. A baby usually weighs only about 4.5 pounds (2 kilograms) at birth. An orangutan mother is very protective of her baby. She seems to stay away from other animals when the baby is very small. Most primates spend a lot of time caring for their babies, grooming them, and feeding them. So do orangutans. Unlike other primates, orangutans almost never play with their babies. They seem to stick to the business of raising the baby.

Baby orangutans weigh about 4.5 pounds (2 kilograms) at birth and are carefully tended by their mothers.

Baby orangutans have pink faces and pink or white circles around their eyes.
They know to stay very close to their mothers.

Occasionally, another lone female joins up with a mother and baby orangutan. This may help a younger female learn how to care for a baby. Females with babies sometimes gather to feed in a rich fruit tree. When these meetings happen, the babies play with each other before following their mothers back to the solitude of the forest. Baby orangutans in zoos may spend much time playing with other babies, but this rarely happens in the wild. Orangutans in the wild, both babies and adults, do not spend much time in play.

For the first year of life the baby must depend on its mother for everything. It clings to its mother's long shaggy fur with its strong toes and fingers. The baby drinks milk from its mother. At about a year of age it begins to eat solid food its mother has chewed and given to the baby.

During this time the baby begins to climb and swing and explore its treetop home, but it is always close to its mother. At about age 7, young orangutans wander off on their own. They may spend some time with other newly independent young adults before they find their own territories and become solitary adults. A young orangutan is not a full-grown adult until its early teen years.

Orangutans
FUNFACT:

A female orangutan will have only 3 or 4 babies in her entire 40-year lifetime.

Mother orangutans spend time taking care of their babies
and on rare occasions play with them.

Baby orangutans have been popular pets in some parts of Southeast Asia. The mother is killed to catch the baby. When they are small, baby orangutans are adorable little clowns. Very soon they grow up and become too large and strong to be kept as pets. This can be a problem. What do people do when their pet orangutan is too big to be a pet any longer? Some people just abandon them. Others try to retrain them to live in the forest again. This is not an easy job and does not always work.

Orangutans
FUNFACT:

Most primates groom not only their babies, but also each other. Orangutans only groom their young.

These two baby Bornean orangutans have been orphaned and are being raised
by people who will try to teach them to live on their own in the wild.

Orangutans build 2 nests each day. One is for napping during the day and one is for sleeping at night.

Nest building is an important behavior for orangutans. Orangutans build 2 nests every day: a day nest for their naps and a night nest. They build their nests in the fork of a tree. They pile thick branches into a sort of a platform, and then they line the center with leaves. A nest may be as large as 5 feet (1.5 meters) around.

Orangutans often pick nest sites that face west to soak up the last warm rays of the setting sun. Sometimes they

Mother orangutans share their nests with their babies until the babies are about 3 years old.

may choose trees that hang over water. This probably gives them better protection from predators. Day nests may be built in trees where orangutans find food. Night nests are never built in feeding trees.

Females always build new nests. Sometimes males or youngsters settle for sleeping in old nests. Young orangutans begin practicing building their own night nests at age 2. They still sleep in their mothers' nests for another year.

Orangutans need the rain forest. It is where they live and find the fruit they eat. Even in a rain forest, fruit is not always easy to find. Scientists have learned that when there is plenty of fruit, orangutans will stuff themselves. They build up the fat in their bodies. That is when they are most likely to mate and have babies. When lots of rich fruit is available, orangutans are also more likely to feed in the same trees as other orangutans.

When there is very little fruit, orangutans eat more leaves, twigs, and nuts.

These foods do not have as many calories (KAL-or-eez) as fruits. Orangutans use up the fat and calories they eat rather than store them. They are more likely to be found alone when there is not enough food to share. Also, orangutans are less likely to mate and have babies when fruit is not plentiful.

When orangutans eat fruit, they help to spread seeds around the forest. This gives new fruit trees a chance to sprout and grow. Without the orangutans, there would be fewer trees. Without the trees, there would be fewer orangutans.

Orangutans
FUNFACT:

When heavy rains come, orangutans build a leafy
ceiling over their heads to protect them.
They use large leaves like an umbrella.

This young orangutan uses leaves as an umbrella during a rainfall.

The future of this young orangutan and of all orangutans depends on people.

The biggest problem facing orangutans is habitat destruction. Many people live in Borneo and Sumatra. Those people turn orangutan forests into cropland for farming and pastureland for their animals to graze. People cut down the forest to grow palm trees in huge plantations. In 1997 and 1998 terrible wildfires in Indonesia destroyed orangutan forests. This left many orangutans homeless, and many baby orangutans became orphans.

There is still a lot to be learned about orangutans. It is very hard to study them in the wild. Orangutans are secretive and so well camouflaged that it is hard to know where they are living in a forest.

The first scientist to study orangutans spent months searching for them, but only got to watch them for 6 hours in all that time. The work of scientists is very important to the survival of orangutans. The more that people can learn about orangutans, the easier it will be to find ways to save them. Knowledge will be the key to saving orangutans.

Orangutans
FUNFACT:

Many places where orangutans live are hard to get to because of steep hillsides, big rivers, and huge jungle trees.

Internet Sites

You can find out more interesting information about orangutans and lots of other wildlife by visiting these Internet sites.

www.animal.discovery.com/	Animal Planet.com
www.animaltime.net/primates/	Aye-Aye's Primate Primer
www.careforthewild.org/animalinfo/orangutan.asp	Care for the Wild International
www.enchantedlearning.com	Enchanted Learning.com
www.fonz.org	Friends of the National Zoo
www.nationalgeographic.com/kids/creature_feature/0102/orangutans2.html	National Geographic Explorer for Kids
www.nwf.org/internationalwildlife/oranguta.html	National Wildlife Federation
www.pbs.org/wnet/nature/orangutans	Nature Series on PBS
www.orangutan.org	Orangutan Foundation International
www.scz.org/animals/o/orang.html	Sedgwick County Zoo
www.panda.org/species/orang	World Wildlife Fund

Index

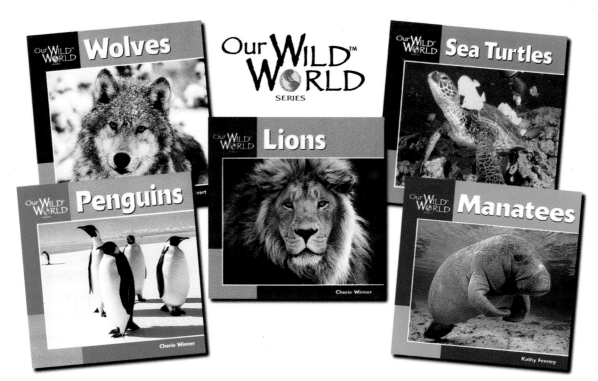

Titles available in the Our Wild World Series:

BISON
ISBN 1-55971-775-0

BLACK BEARS
ISBN 1-55971-742-4

CARIBOU
ISBN 1-55971-812-9

CHIMPANZEES
ISBN 1-55971-845-5

COUGARS
ISBN 1-55971-788-2

DOLPHINS
ISBN 1-55971-776-9

EAGLES
ISBN 1-55971-777-7

GORILLAS
ISBN 1-55971-843-9

LEOPARDS
ISBN 1-55971-796-3

LIONS
ISBN 1-55971-787-4

MANATEES
ISBN 1-55971-778-5

MONKEYS
ISBN 1-55971-849-8

MOOSE
ISBN 1-55971-744-0

ORANGUTANS
ISBN 1-55971-847-1

PENGUINS
ISBN 1-55971-810-2

POLAR BEARS
ISBN 1-55971-828-5

SEA TURTLES
ISBN 1-55971-746-7

SEALS
ISBN 1-55971-826-9

SHARKS
ISBN 1-55971-779-3

TIGERS
ISBN 1-55971-797-1

WHALES
ISBN 1-55971-780-7

WHITETAIL DEER
ISBN 1-55971-743-2

WOLVES
ISBN 1-55971-748-3

See your nearest bookseller, or order by phone 1-800-328-3895

NORTHWORD PRESS
Chanhassen, Minnesota